Our Place, Their Place

Written by Susan Brocker
Illustrated by Marjorie Scott

South Africa

My name is Thabo. I live in Nelspruit, South Africa. Many tourists travel through here to get to the world famous Kruger National Park. Animals are protected in Kruger National Park. But cheetahs and other predators that hunt outside the park boundaries can be a problem for farmers and their livestock.

Contents

Jabu and the Cheetah   4

    The Hungry Cat   4

    Sharing the Land   6

    Guard Dogs   8

    The New Puppy   10

    The Cheetah Returns   12

What's the Problem?   14

Living Together   16

Peace Parks that Protect   18

Sharing Around the World   20

What's Your Opinion?   22

Think Tank   24

Index   24

Look for the **Thinking Cap**.
When you see this picture, you will find
a problem to think about and write about.

Jabu and the Cheetah

The Hungry Cat

The cheetah slunk silently through the long grass. She could see sheep grazing by a watering hole. She was very hungry.

She snuck out of the grass and moved closer. A sheepherder and his son were guarding the sheep. That was their job. They needed the sheep to sell later. Every time a sheep died, they lost money. So they tried hard to keep all of their family's sheep safe.

Suddenly, the sheepherder saw the cheetah. His first reaction was to panic. He had to protect his sheep! "Jabu, run and grab my gun," he yelled at his son.

grazing eating small amounts of food throughout the day

"No!" Jabu cried out. "Please, do not hurt her."
Jabu shouted loudly at the cheetah, "Go! Run!"

The cheetah looked at him with frightened eyes.
She turned quickly and ran. She ran faster than Jabu
had ever seen an animal run before.

Sharing the Land

"Jabu, why did you do that?" his father asked him.
"That cheetah was hunting our sheep."

"Cheetahs are beautiful animals," Jabu said.
"We should not kill them." He told his father about
a tame cheetah that had visited his school.

"They are very gentle. There are hardly any left
in the wild because farmers shoot and trap them."

"But they kill our sheep and goats. We need our
livestock to live," his father said.

"There are ways we can learn to live together
and share the land," Jabu said.

Guard Dogs

Jabu told his father about the battle to save the fastest land animal on Earth.

"People are training special dogs to guard livestock," Jabu said. "The dogs scare the cheetahs away. Then farmers like us do not have to kill them. Can we get one of these dogs, father?" Jabu begged him.

The cheetah is the fastest land animal on Earth. It can reach a speed of 70 miles per hour.

Jabu's father thought about the cheetah. He thought about her beautiful, spotted coat. He thought about her elegant head and teardrop eyes. He thought about her racing across the grasslands at amazing speed.

"You are right, son. Cheetahs are beautiful animals," he said. "We will find out about these guard dogs."

The New Puppy

Shumba, an Anatolian shepherd puppy, arrived at the farm one fine, hot day. He was only eight weeks old and already the size of a small sheep. His trainer said that he must live, eat, sleep, and travel with the sheep from now on.

"This way, he will bond with the herd and become part of their family. Then he will want to protect them," she explained.

The trainer told Jabu and his father that these dogs had been used in Turkey for thousands of years. They guarded herds of goats, sheep, and cattle from wolves and bears. Now they work in Africa to protect livestock from predators such as cheetahs and leopards. The dogs are not trained to attack. Their job is to bark and scare the predators away.

predator an animal that hunts other animals for food

The Cheetah Returns

Shumba grew into a big, strong dog. Jabu and his father herded the sheep onto the grasslands. They left Shumba to watch them. Shumba loved his job and his herd of sheep. Jabu liked to see him standing guard, his black nose pointing into the breeze.

One day, Jabu and his father saw the cheetah again. She slunk out of the bush and sprinted toward the sheep. The breeze was at her back. She did not see or smell Shumba. But Shumba saw and smelled her right away. He rushed in front of his herd, barking loudly at the cheetah. She took one look at the big, strong dog and then turned and ran. Jabu's father smiled. He did not need his gun.

Put On Your Thinking Cap

Write down your thoughts on these questions. Then share your ideas with a classmate.

1. Every country in the world has its own **endangered** wild animals. Find out which wild animals are at risk in your country. Why are they at risk?

2. In what ways can these animals be protected?

3. Which ideas do you think would work best? Why?

Only between 10,000 and 15,000 cheetahs remain in the wild. Cheetahs are very difficult to breed in zoos.

endangered at risk of dying out completely

What's the Problem?

South Africa is home to some of the world's most amazing wild animals, from speedy cheetahs to lumbering elephants. There is a problem, however. The human population of South Africa is growing. More people need more land for farms and homes. They are moving into areas where wild animals once lived. They are driving out the wild animals, leaving them homeless.

Sometimes hungry animals attack farmers' cattle and sheep. Sometimes they damage or eat farmers' crops. The farmers might kill the wild animals to protect their livestock and crops. Many of these wild animals are now endangered.

Animals in Danger

- South Africa is famous for its large, grazing herbivores, such as elephants, rhinoceroses, giraffes, and antelope. It is also famous for its large carnivores, such as cheetahs, lions, leopards, and wild dogs.

- Many of these animals, including cheetahs, wild dogs, elephants, and black rhinoceroses, are now endangered.

- They are at risk mainly because they have fewer places to live. People have turned their grassland homes into farmland. There is less room for the animals to graze or hunt.

Did You Know?

A herbivore is an animal that eats mostly plants.

A carnivore is an animal that eats mostly meat.

15

Living Together

Many people in South Africa are trying to learn ways of sharing their land with wild animals. They are learning about wild animals and their needs. They are building fences and guarding their farms to protect their crops and livestock instead of killing the wild animals.

They are also setting aside areas of land as national parks and reserves where wild animals can live in safety. Instead of farming the land, some people are learning how to earn a living from ecotourism. Visitors from around the world come to see the animals. This brings money into the communities and creates jobs.

ecotourism tourist activities based on respect for nature

Tourists from around the world pay to see wild animals in South Africa's national parks. The money is used to help run the parks and to care for the animals. It is also used to improve the lives of people living nearby.

Put On Your Thinking Cap

Write down your thoughts on these questions. Then share your ideas with a classmate.

1. Can you imagine sharing land with wild animals such as lions and elephants? What might happen when wild animals come close to farms and homes?

2. What do you think could happen to crops and livestock?

3. What do you think could happen to the wild animals?

4. How could the problems be solved?

Peace Parks that Protect

A white rhino is led to the safety of the Great Limpopo Transfrontier Park.

South Africa and some other African nations are working to create huge, safe "peace parks," or protected areas, that cross national borders. Wild animals are free to move from park to park, and from country to country, in safety. Local people are involved in running the parks. African nations are learning to work together to save wild animals.

In 2002, African leaders signed an international treaty setting up the biggest peace park so far, the Great Limpopo Transfrontier Park. It links national parks in South Africa, Zimbabwe, and Mozambique. It covers an area of more than 13,500 square miles.

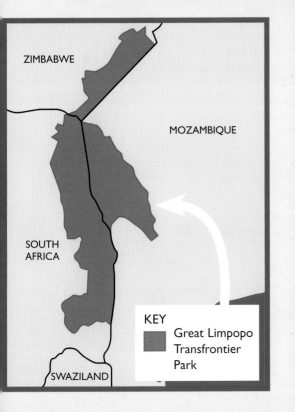

ZIMBABWE

MOZAMBIQUE

SOUTH
AFRICA

SWAZILAND

KEY

Great Limpopo
Transfrontier
Park

Working With Wild Animals

Many Africans, including some former poachers, now work as guides and wardens in the wildlife parks across Africa. They protect the wild animals living in the parks from poaching. They also care for sick, injured, or orphaned wild animals. These are just two of many jobs created when national parks are formed. Can you think of any others?

A tourist and a guide get a close-up view of a cheetah, which is used to seeing humans on the reserve.

poacher someone who catches or kills an animal illegally

19

Sharing Around the World

Wild Wolves

UNITED STATES – In Yellowstone National Park, wolves have been returned to the wild. At first, farmers feared the wolves would kill their sheep and cattle. However, an animal rights group called Defenders of Wildlife pays farmers for any livestock lost. Now farmers are happier to share the land.

Places for Pandas

CHINA – Giant pandas live in the bamboo forests of China. The Chinese government has created protected reserves to help save them. The reserves are linked by corridors of bamboo. Now the pandas can move between the reserves to find food and mates.

Saving a Continent

ANTARCTICA – The frozen continent of Antarctica is one big reserve. Forty-five countries have signed an agreement called the Antarctic Treaty, which protects the plants and animals that live there. Scientists are the only people who are allowed to live and work in Antarctica.

Last-Minute Rescue

BRAZIL – Golden lion tamarins live in the Amazonian rainforests. These monkeys were nearly wiped out as people cut down forests for timber and farming. The Brazilian government paid landowners to create private reserves where golden lion tamarins can live.

Tiger Patrols

INDIA – Special wildlife areas in Asia have been set aside for tigers. Local people patrol the reserves, watching out for poachers. There are large fines for those caught killing tigers. Money from "tiger tourism" helps build local schools and also hospitals.

What's Your Opinion?

Worldwide, the human population is growing. We are needing more land to live on and to grow our food. We are cutting down forests and clearing land for farming. The areas available for wild animals to live in are shrinking.

- Should people be made to give up the land and leave wild animals to live in peace? Why? State your opinion.

- Should the needs of people come before the needs of wild animals? Why or why not?

- What are some ways people can share the land with wild animals?

I think that all animals and plants in the world are connected. We depend on one another to survive. When one living thing dies out, it hurts all living things, including people. It is important to try to save the animals that share our world.

People who kill endangered animals or illegally clear land should go to prison. We must save the animals. We must learn to share our world with them. If these animals die out, we will lose them forever. It makes me very sad to think this could happen.

Many people around the world are very poor. They have to chop down trees to grow food. It's easy for people in rich countries to talk about saving wild animals when they have plenty to eat. But my mom says that people in some of these richer countries also killed wild animals and destroyed their homes a long time ago. So, we have no right to tell poorer people how to live.

Think Tank

1 Around the world, more and more people need land for homes and for growing food. How do you think this affects the local wildlife?

2 In wildlife parks, animals are protected and tourists can travel there to see the animals. This means the local people have an interest in protecting the animals. What else can be done to benefit people and protect wildlife?

Find out more about wildlife issues around the world and how people are working to solve problems. Visit www.researchit.org on the Web.

Index

cheetahs 4–6, 8–10, 12–15, 19

dogs 8–10, 12, 15

endangered animals 13–15, 23

livestock 6, 8, 10, 14, 16–17, 20

poaching 19, 21

reserves and wildlife parks 16–21, 24

tourists 16–17, 19, 24